QUICK FUN

JEWELRY

LEISURE ARTS, INC. • Maumelle, Arkansas

Tassel Necklace

SHOPPING LIST

- ☐ white satin cord
- ☐ white embroidery floss
- ☐ 4 10mm plastic beads (2 white and 2 pink with silver dots)
- ☐ 12mm plastic bead (pink with silver dots)
- ☐ 8mm silver jump ring
- ☐ 3 1/2" square of cardboard
- ☐ 2 pair of chain-nose pliers

To make the Necklace:

1. Make a tassel ***(Fig. 1)*** by wrapping the cardboard about 26 times with embroidery floss and slipping an open jump ring ***(Fig. 2)*** through the tassel top before cutting through the tassel bottom; close the jump ring.

Fig. 1

Fig. 2

*Do the opposite to close.

2. Working just under the jump ring, tightly wrap a 12" length of floss around the tassel several times and tie a knot ***(Fig. 3)***; trim ends even with the tassel.

Fig. 3

3. Dip the tassel into warm water, being careful not to get the wrapped area and top of tassel wet. Lay flat to dry (this allows the floss strands to lie straight). Trim the tassel to 3" long.

4. Cut a 32" length of satin cord. Fold the cord in half; attach to the jump ring with a Lark's Head Knot ***(Fig. 4)***.

Fig. 4

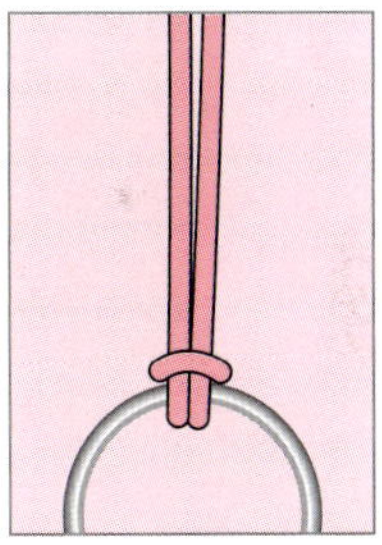

5. Thread the 12mm pink bead onto both cords. Thread 1 white and 1 pink 10mm bead on each cord.

6. Tie the cord ends together with an Overhand Knot ***(Fig. 5)***; trim ends.

Fig. 5

Stretchy Bracelets

SHOPPING LIST

- ☐ black 6mm round faceted beads
- ☐ black pony beads
- ☐ natural wood 8mm rondelle beads
- ☐ large bead for bead stop
- ☐ stretch cord
- ☐ jeweler's glue

To make the Black Bracelet:

1. Cut a 12" length of cord. Place a bead stop ***(Fig. 1)*** at one end of the cord.

Fig. 1

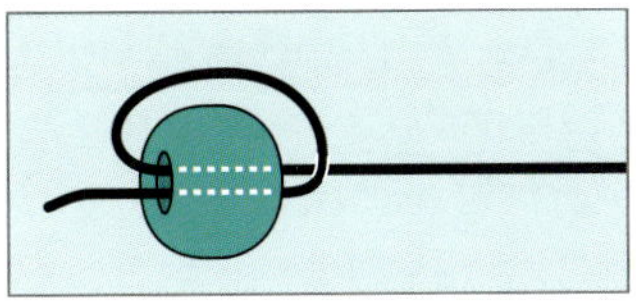

2. Thread black faceted beads on the cord. Check the bracelet size, add or remove beads until the bracelet is the desired length.

3. Remove the bead stop. Tie the cord ends with a surgeon's knot ***(Fig. 2)*** and apply a drop of glue to the knot. Once dry, trim the cord ends.

Fig. 2

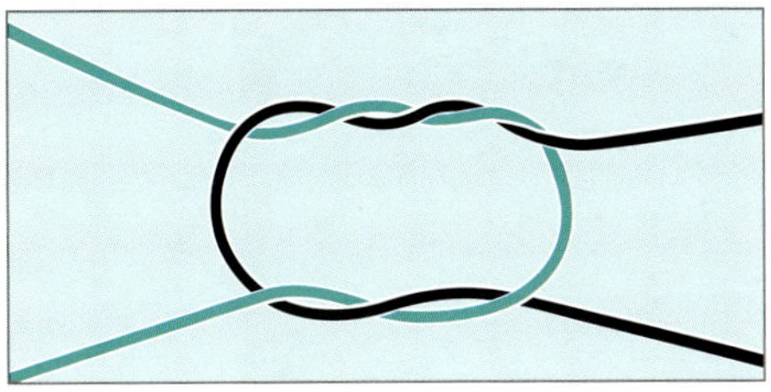

To make the Black/Natural Bracelet:

1. Cut a 12" length of cord. Place a bead stop ***(Fig. 1)*** at one end of the cord.

2. Thread 4 rondelle beads and 1 pony bead on the cord. Ending with a pony bead, repeat the beading pattern until the bracelet is the desired length.

3. Remove the bead stop. Tie the cord ends with a surgeon's knot ***(Fig. 2)*** and apply a drop of glue to the knot. Once dry, trim the cord ends.

Tassel Earrings

SHOPPING LIST

- ☐ silver hoop earrings
- ☐ embroidery floss
- ☐ 2 8mm silver jump rings
- ☐ 2" square of cardboard
- ☐ 2 pair of chain-nose pliers

To make each Earring:

1. Make a tassel ***(Fig. 1)*** by wrapping the cardboard about 30 times with embroidery floss and slipping an open jump ring ***(Fig. 2)*** through the tassel top before cutting through the tassel bottom; close the jump ring.

Fig. 1

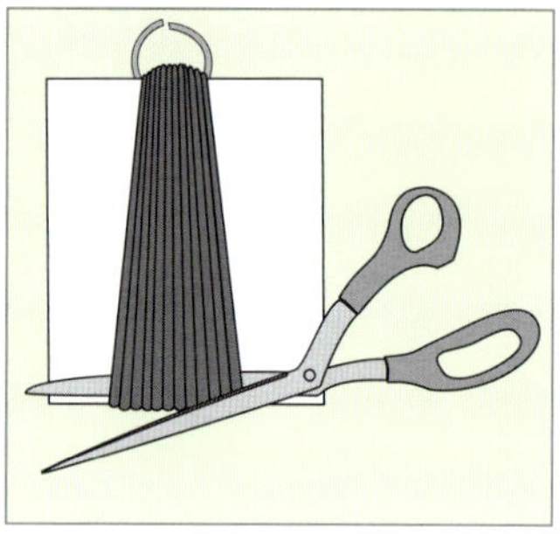

Fig. 2

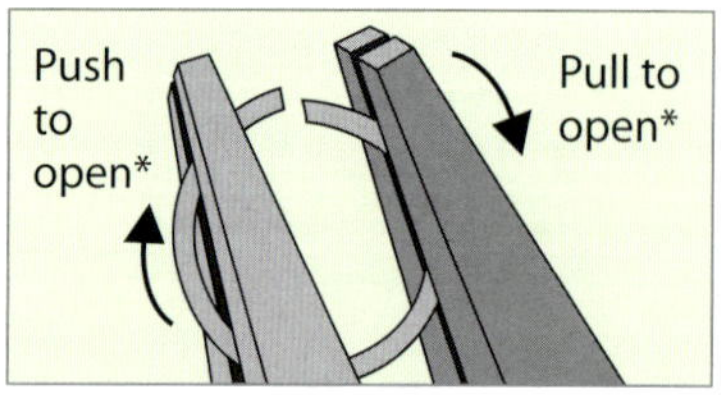

*Do the opposite to close.

2. Working just under the jump ring, tightly wrap a 12" length of floss around the tassel several times and tie a knot ***(Fig. 3)***; trim ends even with the tassel.

Fig. 3

3. Dip the tassel into warm water, being careful not to get the wrapped area and top of tassel wet. Lay flat to dry (this allows the floss strands to lie straight). Trim the tassel to 1" long

4. Slide the tassel on an earring.

Bangle Trio

SHOPPING LIST

- ☐ 3 narrow metal bangle bracelets
- ☐ embroidery floss (white, light blue, and blue)
- ☐ 3 silver ocean-themed charms
- ☐ 33 12mm silver jump rings
- ☐ craft glue

To make each Bracelet:

1. Using glue to adhere the floss at the beginning and end, tightly wrap the bracelet with floss.

2. Use the chain-nose pliers to attach one charm to a jump ring ***(Fig. 1)***; attach the jump ring to the bracelet. Attach 10 more jump rings to the bracelet.

Fig. 1

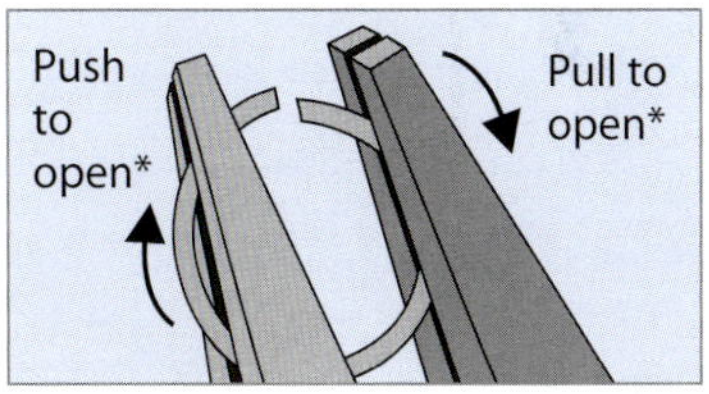

*Do the opposite to close.

Jumbo Craft Stick Bracelets

SHOPPING LIST

- ☐ 2 jumbo craft sticks
- ☐ embroidery floss (green variegated and fushia)
- ☐ container of warm water
- ☐ drinking glass
- ☐ strong rubber bands
- ☐ 3 acrylic jewels (green version)
- ☐ craft glue

To make the Green Bracelet:

1. Place a craft stick in warm water; allow to soak for about 2 hours. Remove the stick from water and test to see if it is soft and pliable. If it is not, return the stick to the water and re-check every 30 minutes until the stick bends easily.

2. Bend the stick around the glass and secure with a rubber band; allow to dry for 24 hours. Remove the bracelet from the glass.

3. On the wrong side, glue a floss end to the bracelet about 1 1/4" from one end. Make closely-spaced vertical wraps around the bracelet, stopping about 1 1/4" from the other end. Glue the floss to the wrong side of the bracelet; cut floss.

4. Spacing about 1/2" apart, glue the jewels to the center front of the bracelet.

To make the Fushia Bracelet:

1. Follow Steps 1-2 of the Green Bracelet.

2. On the wrong side, glue a floss end to the bracelet about 1 1/4" from one end. Make closely-spaced vertical wraps around the bracelet, stopping about 1 1/4" from the other end. Glue the last wrap to the wrong side of the bracelet; do not cut floss.

3. Working toward the starting point, wrap the bracelet with widely-spaced diagonal wraps that lean to the left and right to form diamonds. Glue the last wrap to the wrong side of the bracelet; cut the floss.

Braided Necklace

SHOPPING LIST

- ☐ 3 $2^{1}/_{2}$" x 40" strips of cotton fabric (we used light pink, dark pink, and yellow)
- ☐ 3 32 mm round large-hole wood beads (we used 1 dark pink and 2 yellow beads)
- ☐ 2 12" lengths of embroidery floss to match one fabric (we used yellow)
- ☐ tape

To make the Necklace:

1. With short ends aligned, tape the fabric strips to your work surface. About 3" from the ends, tightly wrap and then tie one floss length around the fabric strips.

2. Tightly braid ***(Fig. 1)*** the strips for about 27". Wrap and tie the remaining floss length around the fabric strips. Trim the fabric strip tails to about 3".

Fig. 1

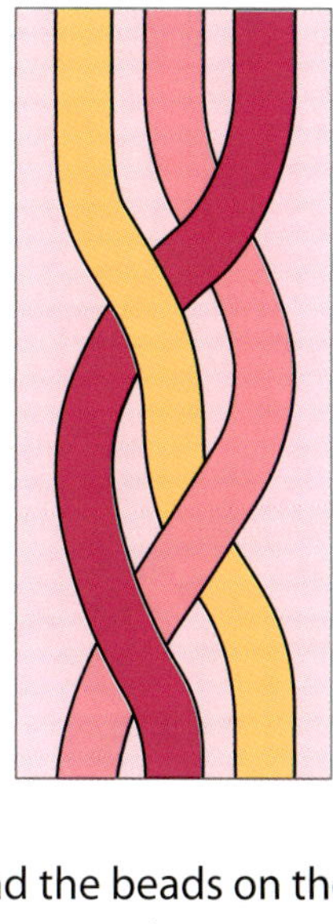

3. Thread the beads on the braid until centered. To wear, tie the ends together.

Fabric-Wrapped Bangle

SHOPPING LIST

- ☐ 1$^{1}/_{2}$" wide wood bangle bracelet
- ☐ 1$^{1}/_{4}$" x 40" - 42" strip of cotton fabric
- ☐ craft glue

To make the Bangle:

1. Glue the wrong side of one end of the fabric strip to the inside of the bangle.

2. Overlapping each previous wrap by about $^{1}/_{2}$", wrap the fabric strip around the bangle; glue the fabric end to the inside of the bangle.

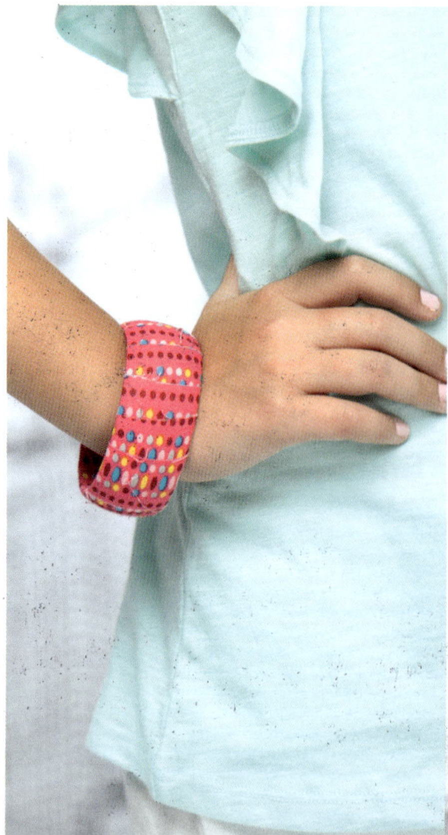

Puzzle Necklaces

SHOPPING LIST

- ☐ 2 24" long ball chains with a connecter
- ☐ 2 cardboard puzzle pieces
- ☐ scrap of scrapbook paper
- ☐ craft glue
- ☐ craft knife and cutting mat
- ☐ 1/8" hole punch

To make each Necklace:

1. Cut a square of scrapbook paper slightly larger than the puzzle piece.
2. Apply glue to the paper back and place on the puzzle piece. Smooth the paper in place; allow glue to dry.
3. Place the puzzle piece wrong side up on the cutting mat. Use the craft knife to carefully trim the excess paper from the puzzle piece.
4. Punch a hole in one "leg" of the puzzle piece. Open the connector and slide the puzzle piece on the chain; close connector.

Safety Pin Bracelet

SHOPPING LIST

- ☐ $1^1/_2$" safety pins (we used 46 for a 6" bracelet)
- ☐ assorted round and cylindrical wood mini beads
- ☐ 2 large beads for bead stops
- ☐ stretch cord
- ☐ jeweler's glue
- ☐ tape

To make the Bracelet:

1. Slide 5-8 assorted beads on each safety pin; close the pin.

2. Cut two 12" lengths of cord. Place a bead stop ***(Fig. 1)*** at one end of each cord. Spacing the cords about 1" apart, tape the cords to your work surface. Keeping the cords parallel as you work, alternately thread round beads and beaded safety pins on the cords ***(Fig. 2)***.

Fig. 1

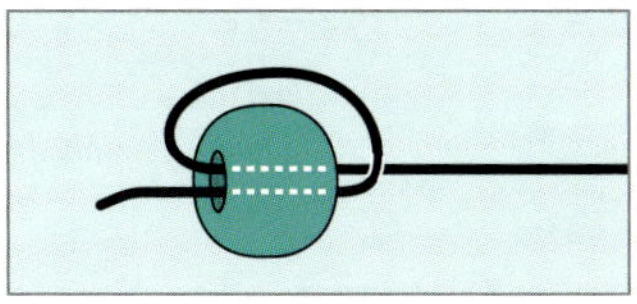

Fig. 2

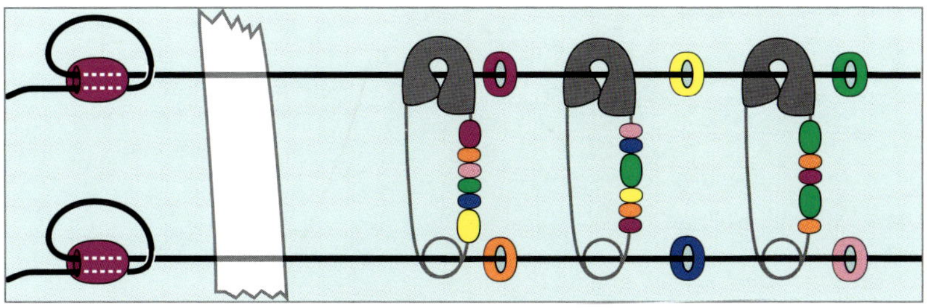

3. Check the bracelet size, adding or removing beads and safety pins until the bracelet is the desired length. Remove the bead stops. Tie the cord ends with a surgeon's knot (***(Fig. 3)*** and apply a drop of glue to each knot. Once dry, trim the cord ends.

Fig. 3

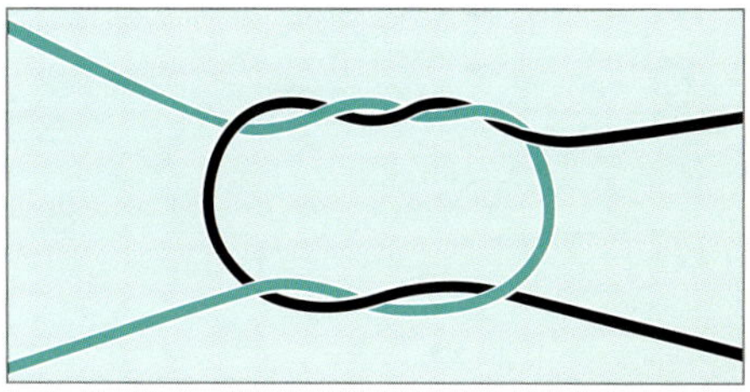

Mini Craft Stick Bracelets

SHOPPING LIST

- ☐ brown waxed cotton cord
- ☐ 2 mini craft sticks
- ☐ brown and green extra-fine-point permanent markers (flower design)
- ☐ washi tape (multi-color design)
- ☐ container of warm water
- ☐ drinking glass or small glass jar
- ☐ strong rubber bands
- ☐ craft knife and cutting mat
- ☐ ice pick or awl

To make the Flower Bracelet:

1. Place a craft stick in warm water; allow to soak for about one hour. Remove the stick from water and test to see if it is soft and pliable. If it is not, return the stick to the water and re-check every 30 minutes until the stick bends easily.

2. Use the awl or ice pick to make a hole about 1/8" from each end of the craft stick.

3. Bend the craft stick around the glass or jar so there is a slight curve to the stick and secure with a rubber band; allow to dry for 24 hours. Remove the rubber band and craft stick from the glass. ***Tip:*** Another option to curve the craft stick is to bend the wet stick to fit *inside* the glass and allow to dry.

4. Use the permanent markers to draw 4 flowers on the craft stick.

5. Cut two 12" cord lengths. Fold one cord in half and attach to the stick using a Lark's Head Knot ***(Fig. 1)***. Repeat with the remaining cord.

Fig. 1

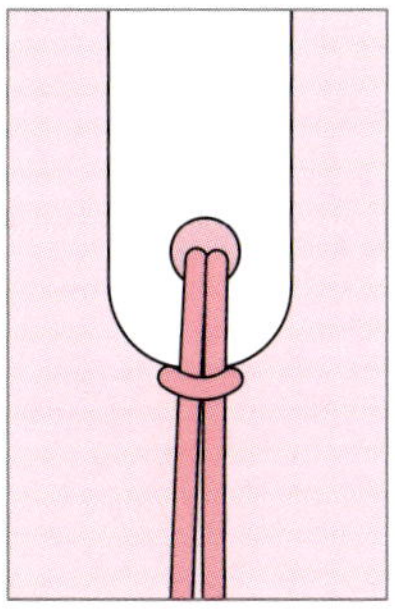

6. To close the bracelet with sliding knots, overlap the cord ends by about 3". Tie an Overhand Knot with each end around the cords on the opposite side ***(Fig. 2)***.

Fig. 2

To make the Multi-color Bracelet:

1. Follow Steps 1-3 of the Flower Bracelet.

2. Cut a piece of washi tape the length of the craft stick. Adhere the tape piece to the craft stick. Use the craft knife to carefully trim the tape even with the edges of the craft stick. Use the awl or ice pick to make holes in the tape to match the holes in the stick.

3. Follow Steps 5-6 of Flower Bracelet.

Wood Pendant Necklace

SHOPPING LIST

- ☐ rainbow hemp jewelry cord
- ☐ 2 14mm aqua swirl wood beads
- ☐ 36mm wood ring

To make the Necklace:

1. Cut a 30" length of cord.

2. Fold the cord in half; attach the cord to the wood ring with a Lark's Head Knot ***(Fig. 1)***.

Fig. 1

3. About 1" above the wood ring, tie an Overhand Knot ***(Fig. 2)*** in each cord. Thread a bead on each cord and tie an Overhand Knot.

Fig. 2

4. Tie the cord ends together with an Overhand Knot; trim ends.

Production Team: Technical Writer – Jean Lewis; Technical Associate – Mary Sullivan Hutcheson; Editorial Writer – Susan Frantz Wiles; Senior Graphic Artist – Lora Puls; Graphic Artist – Kellie McAnulty; Photostylist – Lori Wenger; Photographer – Jason Masters.

Made in U.S.A.